ELLEN OCHOA

CLAUDIA ROMO EDELMAN
AND NATHALIE ALONSO

ILLUSTRATED BY **MANUEL GUTIERREZ**

ROARING BROOK PRESS

NEW YORK

For my mom,
who lost her battle to COVID,
but whose values live in me every day. I am
who I am because she was the best of role models.

For my husband, Richard, and children, Joshua and Tamara,
who surround me with their love, their belief in me,
and support. They make it all possible.

Most of all, this series is dedicated to the children
of tomorrow. We know that you have to see it to
be it. We hope these Latinx heroes teach you
to spread your wings and fly.

—C. R. E.

For you, young reader. May these pages inspire
your own bold, beautiful life story.

—N. A.

Published by Roaring Brook Press
Roaring Brook Press is a division of Holtzbrinck Publishing Holdings Limited Partnership
120 Broadway, New York, NY 10271 • mackids.com

Our books may be purchased in bulk for promotional, educational, or business use. Please contact your local bookseller or the Macmillan Corporate and Premium Sales Department at (800) 221-7945 ext. 5442 or by email at MacmillanSpecialMarkets@macmillan.com.

Library of Congress Cataloging-in-Publication Data is available.

First edition, 2023
Book design by Julia Bianchi
Printed in the United States of America by Lakeside Book Company, Crawfordsville, Indiana

ISBN 978-1-250-82828-6 (paperback)
10 9 8 7 6 5 4 3 2 1

ISBN 978-1-250-82827-9 (hardcover)
10 9 8 7 6 5 4 3 2 1

CHAPTER ONE

A LOVE OF MUSIC AND MATH

"What everyone in the astronaut corps shares in common is not gender or ethnic background, but motivation, perseverance, and desire—the desire to participate in a voyage of discovery."

—ELLEN OCHOA

Ellen Ochoa brought her flute to her lips. She had been playing the flute for twenty-five years, and like she'd done so many times, she blew into the mouthpiece and moved her fingers on the keys to create a melody. However, this performance was unlike any she had ever given before or would ever give again.

Ordinarily, Ellen might have been practicing on her own or under the guidance of a teacher. She might even have been playing a solo in a concert hall in front of an audience of music aficionados. But this time, there wasn't even solid ground beneath her feet.

Instead, she was in orbit 160 miles above the earth in a space shuttle called *Discovery*, a machine unlike any other humankind had ever built. The white-and-blue orb spun outside the windows as Ellen played for four fellow astronauts. Without any sheet music to guide her, she filled the spacecraft's cabin with songs she knew by heart—like the hymns of the US Marine Corps and the US Navy, and tunes by the classical artists Mozart and Vivaldi.

"It's a very fond memory," Ellen told CNN years later. "It was just very peaceful."

In April 1993 Ellen Ochoa became the first astronaut ever to play the flute in low orbit around the earth. Playing the flute inside a space shuttle was not so different from playing here on Earth, except for one significant detail: To play the instrument, Ellen had to insert her feet inside loops that were attached to *Discovery*'s floor. Otherwise the microgravity (gravity, the force that keeps us on the ground, is almost nonexistent in space) would have made her float and bounce about the cabin! Even with her feet secure in the loops, Ellen could still feel the force of blowing into the flute make her gently sway.

On that flight, Ellen achieved a greater distinction than

playing the flute in orbit. As the granddaughter of Mexican immigrants, she made history as the first woman of Hispanic descent to travel to outer space. After years of hard work and perseverance, she had beaten the odds to turn a dream that had once seemed impossible into a reality. And in doing so, she would show many people like her that they, too, could accomplish things that were out of this world.

Ellen Lauri Ochoa was born on May 10, 1958, in Los Angeles, California, to Joseph and Rosanne Ochoa. Many years would pass before the idea of becoming an astronaut and going into space would first cross her mind. Historic events in the months before and after Ellen's birth, however, would lead her life toward the stars—literally.

Ellen was born during a time of high tensions between the United States and its rival on the global stage, the Soviet Union (now Russia). The tensions began in the late 1940s, when both nations became the world's two superpowers following the end of World War II. This period of tension between the United States and Russia was known as the Cold War because the two countries competed for political influence around the world without engaging in direct military battles against each other. The Cold War lasted until December 1991, when the Soviet Union collapsed.

During the early years of the Cold War, both the United States and the Soviet Union became fascinated with exploring outer space. That fascination ballooned into an obsession that quickly escalated into a competition, as both countries poured enormous amounts of money into their space-exploration programs. Each nation was driven to make the most progress in this new and exciting frontier of science. This fierce competition, which would become known as the Space Race, would engross not just the United States and the Soviet Union but also the entire world. And like in any race, spectators and rivals alike were captivated to see who would be the first.

Both the countries aspired to send people to space. But before they could do that, their scientists needed to learn how to send *machines* into space to support human endeavors. At the beginning of the Space Race, the Soviet Union got the upper hand. In October 1957, less than a year before Ellen's birth, the Soviets made history when they launched *Sputnik 1*, the world's first artificial satellite—a human-made object that orbits the earth. This marked the beginning of the Space Age, a period of major breakthroughs in space exploration. Just a month after launching *Sputnik 1*, the Soviet Union made history again when it launched a second satellite, *Sputnik 2*. On board was a dog named Laika, who became the first animal launched into space.

The success of *Sputnik 1* and *Sputnik 2* caught the United States by surprise and embarrassed the nation. Not to be outdone by the Soviet Union, the United States felt the need to respond quickly. But the country's first attempt to launch its own satellite into orbit around the earth was another major embarrassment. In December 1957, just two months after the launch of *Sputnik 2*, the United States rushed to put a satellite called *Vanguard TV-3* into orbit. The launch of *Vanguard TV-3* from Cape Canaveral on the eastern coast of Florida was broadcast live on television—only for the aircraft to explode when it was barely four feet above the ground. Newspapers around the world made fun of the United States by giving the failed launch nicknames—"Flopnik" and "Kaputnik."

After that humiliating moment, the US government gave

the California Institute of Technology's Jet Propulsion Laboratory a challenge: to design and build a new satellite as fast as possible. In just three months, that new satellite, called *Explorer 1*, was ready to take off. On January 31, 1958, the United States officially entered the Space Age when the US Army successfully launched *Explorer 1*, the first satellite to carry scientific instruments into space, into orbit.

THE SIGNIFICANCE OF *EXPLORER 1*

EXPLORER 1 was not just a milestone for the United States; it also led scientists to discover the Van Allen belts, which are a pair of doughnut-shaped rings of electrons and other charged particles, or radiation, that surround Earth. These particles are held in place by Earth's magnetic field. The existence of the Van Allen belts was confirmed by another satellite, *Explorer 3*, which the United States launched in March 1958. It was a major discovery because radiation in large quantities is harmful to humans. Therefore, if they ever wanted to send humans into deep space, scientists would have to figure out how to get astronauts past the radiation of the Van Allen belts safely.

Then, on July 29, when Ellen was not yet three months old, something even bigger happened: President Dwight D. Eisenhower signed the National Aeronautics and Space Act of 1958 into law, creating the National Aeronautics and Space Administration (NASA), an agency dedicated to space exploration. NASA's primary goal was to send humans to space, and its creation showed how determined the United States was to beat the Soviet Union in the Space Race.

As a result, Ellen grew up at a time when the Space Race was everywhere, all the time—on television, on the radio, on the front pages of newspapers. It was impossible to ignore. On April 12, 1961, the Soviet Union scored another important victory when one of its cosmonauts (as astronauts in Russia are known), Yuri Gagarin, became the first human in space when he orbited Earth aboard the spacecraft *Vostok 1*. When it came to human spaceflight, the Soviet Union was beating the United States hands down.

On May 5, 1961, less than a month after Gagarin made history for the Soviet Union and five days before Ellen celebrated her third birthday, Alan Shepard became the first American and the second person to travel to space. However, he did not orbit Earth, so despite this great milestone, many Americans felt that the United States was losing the

Space Race. That feeling only got worse in August of that year, when another Soviet cosmonaut, Gherman Titov, became the second human to orbit Earth.

Anxious to beat the Soviet Union at something, then president John F. Kennedy declared that the United States would land a man on the moon—and soon. In an address to the US Congress on May 25, 1961, he said, "I believe that this nation should commit itself to achieving the goal, before this decade is out, of landing a man on the moon and returning him safely to Earth."

The United States fulfilled a major step toward this ambitious goal almost immediately. On February 20, 1962, after Kennedy's speech to Congress, US astronaut John Glenn finally became the first American to orbit Earth. Approximately 135 million people—the largest television audience in history at that time—watched John's spacecraft, the *Friendship 7* capsule, take off from Florida's Cape Canaveral, which had become established as the launch site for NASA missions. Thousands gathered along the coast of Florida to see the capsule take off in person.

After circling the planet three times, John safely splashed down into the Atlantic Ocean, near the Turks and Caicos Islands, and was pulled out of the water by the US Navy. His successful mission was a huge moment for the

United States in the Space Race, and he was hailed as a hero by Americans across the country. Parades were held in his honor in New York City and in his hometown of New Concord, Ohio. But soon, all eyes would be on the moon.

At Rice University in Houston, Texas, in September 1962, President Kennedy delivered another speech about the country's plans for visiting the moon. "We choose to go to the moon in this decade and do the other things, not because they are easy, but because they are hard," the president declared in that famous address. President Kennedy delivered what is now referred to as the moon speech in Houston because the city had been chosen as the site for the Manned Spacecraft Center, the headquarters for NASA's spaceflight program. Construction had already begun the previous April, and this massive complex, which today is known as the Johnson Space Center (JSC), would play a central role in Ellen's life.

Kennedy's challenge led to the creation of NASA's Apollo program, which, in accordance with the president's vision, had the goal of both landing a crew of astronauts on the moon and safely returning them to Earth. The quest to put humans on the moon excited not only scientists but the entire country, including children like Ellen. When a launch took place on a school day for Ellen, a staff member would bring a television into the classroom so that students could watch history unfold.

Soon after she finished sixth grade, eleven-year-old Ellen and her family were among the 650 million people across the globe who gathered around their television sets on July 20, 1969, to watch American astronaut Neil Armstrong become the first man to walk on the moon. Ellen heard Neil utter the famous words, "That's one small step for man, one giant leap for mankind," and saw him plant the US flag on the moon's surface. It had taken NASA just eight years to achieve this extraordinary achievement. And for a country that for much of its history had been, and continues to be, divided, it was a rare moment of national unity and pride.

President Kennedy did not live to see his dream of an American moon landing fulfilled—he was assassinated in Dallas, Texas, in November 1963—but the success of the Apollo program is a big part of his legacy. In fact, after his death, President Lyndon B. Johnson—who Johnson Space Center in Houston is named after—renamed the NASA facilities in Florida that serves as a launch site for space missions as the Kennedy Space Center.

WHAT WAS THE APOLLO PROGRAM?

NASA created the APOLLO PROGRAM in 1961 with the goal of landing humans on the moon and returning them to Earth safely. From 1968 to 1972 there were a total of fourteen Apollo missions, including eleven spaceflights. The first four flights were used to test equipment. In 1968 the Apollo 8 mission orbited the moon, which was a precursor to the first moon landing that occurred in 1969.

Over these four years, a total of twenty-four American astronauts made the journey to the moon and back—and twelve of them even walked across its surface. To this day, the United States is the only country that has landed humans on the moon. By the end of the Apollo program, the United States had spent $25.8 billion, which would be equal to more than $257 billion in today's money.

While they were on the moon, the astronauts studied its surface and brought back pieces of moon rocks—more than eight hundred pounds of rock in total—for scientists on Earth to study. These rocks have helped scientists learn more about what the moon is made of and how and when the moon and Earth were formed.

However, even as she watched these historic events unfold, young Ellen could not imagine ever putting on a spacesuit and blasting into space herself—simply because she was a girl. In its early days, NASA hired only men to be astronauts. When a girl named Linda Halpern wrote a letter to President Kennedy in 1962 expressing her interest in becoming an astronaut, NASA wrote back saying, "We have no present plans to employ women on spaceflights because of the degree of scientific and flight training, and the physical characteristics, which are required."

Even after a Soviet cosmonaut, Valentina Tereshkova, became the first woman to go to outer space in June 1963, a long time passed before NASA gave American women the same opportunity. While some women did work at NASA in various roles during this time, they typically worked behind the scenes.

"A lot of times people ask me, 'Well, during the Apollo program, was this something that you decided to do?' I have to kind of remind folks that, of course, there were no women astronauts at that time—very few who worked at NASA at all," Ellen later said on the Tufts University *Tell Me More* podcast. "So, nobody would ever ask a girl, 'Would you like to grow up to be an astronaut?' It certainly wasn't something I thought of at all."

One of five children, Ellen grew up in La Mesa, a suburb of San Diego. Like many folks in Southern California, Ellen's grandparents on her dad's side of the family were immigrants from Mexico. They had arrived in Arizona from the northern Mexican state of Sonora, located just on the other side of the United States–Mexico border. Later they relocated to California, where Ellen's father, Joseph, was born. He was the youngest of twelve kids. Ellen's mother, Rosanne, was born in Oklahoma and moved to California as a teenager. While Joseph worked as a manager in a department store, Rosanne stayed at home to care for their children.

PROTESTING THE APOLLO PROGRAM

Not all Americans believed it was right for the US government to invest so much money into the Apollo program just to beat the Soviet Union in the Space Race. In July 1969, days before the Apollo 11 mission took off from Cape Canaveral in Florida, Reverend Ralph Abernathy, who had been an aide to civil rights icon Martin Luther King Jr., led a group of about five hundred African American activists to the Kennedy Space Center to protest the moon landing.

With so many families across the country who did not have enough food, water, and clothing, Abernathy and the activists argued that the vast amounts of money the US government was spending on the Apollo program would be better used to solve those problems. Some protesters carried signs that read "$12 a day to feed an astronaut, we could feed a child for $8." The activists also brought a pair of mules and a wooden wagon to create a contrasting image between NASA's expensive spacecraft and the struggles of people who didn't have enough food to eat or proper housing.

The protest reminded Americans that, as exciting as space exploration was, there were still plenty of challenges to be tackled right here on Earth.

Despite his Mexican ancestry, Ellen's father didn't push his children to speak Spanish at home. Although her mother tried to teach Ellen and her siblings some Spanish, Ellen never learned the language. Later, she would realize that her dad had probably been shamed for speaking Spanish—one of the many examples of racism Mexican Americans and other immigrants often experience in the United States—and that that was likely the reason why he had motivated his children to speak only English.

"When my dad was growing up, there were just not very pleasant experiences if you spoke Spanish at that time, and there was a real push to speak English and be part of the English-speaking community," Ellen told journalist Guy Raz on NPR's *Wisdom from the Top* podcast in 2021. "He saw English as being important and Spanish as not something we really needed to learn, which is unfortunate, because it would have been so easy to grow up really quite bilingual."

When Ellen was young, her parents divorced, and Ellen and her siblings lived with their mother, who put a strong emphasis on education. Rosanne Ochoa had a condition known as asthma, which can make it difficult to breathe. Though now there are treatments that allow people with asthma to attend school, go to work, and pursue all types of activities, when Rosanne was young, the condition prevented her from attending high school with other people her age. Instead, she earned a general educational diploma, or GED, which is an alternative to a high school degree.

Rosanne did not attend college as a young woman, either, but she did take courses at San Diego State University—one class at a time—while raising her five children. In fact, Ellen's mom often did her homework alongside her kids. It took her twenty years, but not only did Rosanne earn her bachelor's degree in 1982, she graduated summa cum laude—meaning she was at the top of her class.

Rosanne's emphasis on education was a great source of inspiration for Ellen, who grew up loving to learn. "My mom had the biggest influence on me, encouraging my siblings and me to study hard and showing us her enjoyment of learning," Ellen said in an interview with the National Women's History Museum.

While she was growing up, Ellen was much more interested in music than science. She started playing the flute at ten years old and eventually joined her school's marching and concert bands. Ellen became a standout flutist and even got to perform with the California All-State Honor Band.

Although she took few science classes in high school, teenage Ellen discovered that she really loved math, largely thanks to a teacher, Ms. Paz Jensen.

"Usually, girls weren't encouraged to go to college and major in math and science," Ellen told *La Prensa San Diego*, a Hispanic newspaper. "[Ms. Jensen] made math appealing and motivated me to continue studying it in college."

~~~~~~~~~~~~~~~~~~~

MEXICAN IMMIGRATION TO THE UNITED STATES

Mexicans make up the largest immigrant group in the United States. Because of the proximity between the two nations, the United States is home to the largest number of Mexican people of any other country other than Mexico itself. Mexican influence has enriched American culture with its food, music, art, architecture, language, and literature.

In fact, much of the southwest region of the United States previously belonged to Mexico. The states we know as Utah, Nevada, California, and Arizona, as well as parts of New Mexico, Wyoming, Texas, and Colorado, used to be part of Mexico. The United States acquired those lands in 1848 through an agreement known as the Treaty of Guadalupe Hidalgo, which marked the end of a conflict called the Mexican American War.

When those areas became part of the United States, the Mexican people who were already living in that region were forced to choose between uprooting their lives and moving to lands that still belonged to Mexico or becoming US citizens. At first the US government promised Mexican people who owned this land under Mexican law that they would be able to keep their property. However, this promise was stricken from the Treaty of Guadalupe Hidalgo before the agreement became official.

In another unjust act, US courts also asked Mexican Americans to provide proof that they owned the lands they claimed, which everyone knew was extremely difficult to do. Many of the original landowners did not have the documents to support their cases, nor could they afford to pay lawyers to advocate for their rights to their land. The courts used this as an excuse to deny most of the land claims made by Mexican Americans and deprive these people of their property.

Over decades, the Mexican presence in the United States has continued to grow. Many Mexican workers immigrated to the United States in the late nineteenth century to take jobs in mines and farms in the Southwest. During the Mexican Revolution, from 1910 to 1920, many more came to the United States to flee war and persecution. In 1910 there were approximately twenty thousand people of Mexican origin in the United States. Just ten years later, in 1920, that number was somewhere between fifty thousand and one hundred thousand. Many of these Mexican immigrants were deported, or forced to return to Mexico, during the Great Depression, a period of world-wide economic crisis between 1929 and 1939.

The early years of World War II marked an increase in the number of Mexicans immigrating to the United States due in part to the Bracero Program, which allowed American farmers to temporarily hire Mexican laborers to work on their farms. Other Mexican workers also were hired to work on US railroads. The Bracero Program ran from 1942 to 1962. During this time, these laborers—or braceros—were forced to work long hours and toil under dangerous conditions, live in cramped barracks that did not have enough bathrooms and showers for all the workers, and were not fed well or paid fair wages.

About five million Mexicans came to the United States under the Bracero Program, and while many of them moved back to Mexico when the program ended, hundreds of thousands remained in the United States. But after permitting these Mexican workers to enter the country after World War II to perform the important work of growing food and building infrastructure, the United States deported many undocumented Mexican people who had entered the country hoping to finding jobs, too. American citizens of Mexican descent were among the people the US government rounded up and deported to Mexico by plane, boats, and buses. Instead of their hometowns, many were transported to parts of Mexico that were unfamiliar to them. Imagine being told to go back home only to be taken to a place that is strange to you.

But far from staying silent in the face of injustice, Mexican and Mexican Americans in the United States have rallied to demand rights and fair treatment throughout the years. In the 1960s, Mexican American labor leaders Cesar Chavez and Dolores Huerta founded the National Farm Workers Association (NFWA). The NFWA was an organization created in response to the inhumane treatment that migrant farmworkers experienced. The group brought migrant farmworkers together to achieve better wages and working conditions. The group later became known as the United Farm Workers of America (UFW).

Cesar and Dolores's efforts were part of a broader effort known as the Chicano movement, which saw Mexican Americans unite to secure more political and educational opportunities. They also sought to recover lands that had been seized from Mexican peoples in the years after the Treaty of Guadalupe Hidalgo went into effect.

People from Mexico continue to face hostility in the United States to this day, yet they have flourished, building strong communities in many parts of the country, particularly in California, Texas, and Arizona. Today, Mexicans and Mexican Americans contribute to every field imaginable: education, entertainment, medicine, the military, politics, and much more.

CHAPTER TWO

DISCOVERING THE WONDERS OF STEM

"I know that role models make a difference, and I take seriously that part of my career and life."

—ELLEN OCHOA

Ellen graduated from Grossmont High School in La Mesa, California, in 1975. She was the valedictorian—the top student in her class—and delivered a speech at her graduation. But her days as a student were only beginning. Ellen decided to attend San Diego State University, where her mother took courses. Some of Ellen's older siblings were also students at the same university.

Although she had once thought about studying music in college and playing the flute professionally, Ellen's love of math led her to consider careers in STEM—science, technology, engineering, and mathematics. She took many classes in calculus, one of the most difficult kinds of mathematics.

WHAT IS CALCULUS?

CALCULUS is a field of math that helps us understand the changes that occur during a process. For example, as planets move around the sun along their orbits, their positions change. Calculus helps scientists figure out where a planet will be in its orbit at a given moment, which is important information to know if, let's say, you are sending a spacecraft to fly by a planet to take pictures of it.

Calculus also helps us better understand how quickly changes happen and therefore has many applications here on Earth. For example, epidemiologists—scientists who study disease outbreaks—use calculus to determine how fast a virus or another pathogen might spread. And meteorologists—scientists who study weather—use calculus to make predictions, such as the direction a hurricane might take and how strong it will become. Calculus is critical to many other fields, too, including architecture, engineering, and medicine.

In college, Ellen became interested in electrical engineering, a field that involves creating systems and machines that run on electricity. Unfortunately, at that time, not everyone believed that a woman could work in that field, much less excel in it. As a result of this bias, most electrical engineers were men.

"I went to talk to a professor in the electrical engineering department," Ellen said in an interview with CNBC in 2021. "He made it very clear: He was not interested in having me in his department."

Early in her college career, Ellen considered majoring in music, business administration, or even journalism. But in the end, she chose to pursue a STEM major. Instead of electrical engineering, however, Ellen studied physics—the branch of science that involves matter and the forces that act on it, like gravity. Physics includes many different scientific areas, including mechanics (the study of motion), acoustics (the study of sound), and optics (the study of light). Ellen ended up focusing on optics in college. Although Ellen wasn't thinking about going to space yet—it still was not something women were given the opportunity to do—studying physics would prove to be good preparation for becoming an astronaut.

Luckily, Ellen's physics professors were much more

encouraging of her talents and interests. One professor told her that her knowledge of calculus had been great preparation for studying physics. "He said, 'You'll be way ahead if you've already taken calculus . . . I think you'd do really well,'" Ellen said in an interview with the Adler Planetarium. "So, I think it's not too surprising that I decided to give physics a try."

Still, Ellen noticed how few women—and even fewer women of color—were in her science classes. "When I was going through school, it was pretty unusual for a woman to be in STEM fields. Certainly, any woman of color. In some [classes], I was the only woman. In others, maybe one of two or four. I can only remember one class with more than that," she told CNBC.

While Ellen was in college, important things were happening at NASA that would have an enormous impact on her life and career. The 1970s marked a significant shift in the history of space exploration, including the development of a new type of spacecraft, a marvel of science and engineering—the space shuttle. Previous spacecraft, like the type used during the Apollo program, could only travel to space one time. This was inconvenient because spacecraft are expensive to build. NASA realized that it could get a bigger return on its investments if it could build reusable spacecraft that could travel to space more than once. That new spacecraft was the space shuttle, which was designed to transport both people and cargo into orbit around Earth and back.

The main section of the space shuttle that carried astronauts was called an orbiter. Attached to the outside of the orbiter were a pair of rockets, called boosters, that helped the orbiter gain enough speed to break away from Earth's gravity and get through its atmosphere. Once they ran out of fuel, these boosters fell back down to Earth, into the ocean, where they would be recovered, then reused in future space shuttle launches. The orbiter also had wings, so after taking off from Earth pointing upward, like a rocket ship, and fulfilling its mission, it was capable of landing on a runway—like an airplane.

NASA built four space shuttles: *Atlantis*, *Challenger*, *Columbia*, and *Discovery*, each designed to fly at least one hundred times. These space shuttles were used to conduct experiments in space, launch and repair communication satellites already in orbit around Earth, and help build and transport people and supplies to a large space laboratory known as the International Space Station (ISS), a large spacecraft in permanent orbit around Earth where astronauts can live for extended periods of time and conduct experiments.

In its early days, NASA mostly recruited military test pilots to become astronauts because they are trained to put new aircraft to the test. Therefore, these men not only had flight experience, they had also learned how to react in dangerous situations. In other words, they routinely risked their lives while doing their jobs. But after the invention of the space shuttle, which was created to conduct all sorts of scientific experiments in orbit, NASA found itself in need of experts in many other fields, too. So the agency began expanding its hiring practices to recruit people who had backgrounds in a variety of sciences, including physics and engineering, to become astronauts.

This and another key development at NASA created a new opportunity for Ellen. Because the agency primarily looked to the military to recruit astronauts, it's no surprise that in the first few decades of its existence, it only recruited men, since most members of the military were, and still are, men. But that changed in 1977 when, thanks to the development of the space shuttle, NASA opened the astronaut program to women for the first time. In 1978, six women were among the new class of astronaut candidates selected by the agency, paving the way for more women to leave their mark in space.

"It was certainly very important for me to see women astronauts—it hadn't been possible before that 1978 class, and the first six women demonstrated their skill in a way that helped all the women who came after them," Ellen said in an interview with the National Women's History Museum.

Two years later, in 1980, with her family in attendance, Ellen put on her cap and gown and celebrated her graduation from San Diego State University. Earning her bachelor's degree in physics was an enormous accomplishment, but her education was far from over: Ellen had decided to continue her studies at Stanford University, which is also in California.

1978: A YEAR OF MANY FIRSTS AT NASA

The 1978 NASA ASTRONAUT CLASS, which consisted of a total of thirty-five astronauts, was the most diverse in the agency's history at the time. In addition to six women, it included the first three African American astronauts (Guion "Guy" Bluford, Frederick D. Gregory, and Ronald McNair), the first Asian American astronaut (Ellison S. Onizuka, of Japanese descent), and the first Jewish American astronaut (Judith Resnik).

Meanwhile, at NASA, the space shuttle program was charging ahead. Less than a year after Ellen began her graduate studies at Stanford, *Columbia* became the first space shuttle orbiter to fly and thus began a new era in space exploration. It launched on April 12, 1981, from Kennedy Space Center in Florida with two astronauts on board, marking the first time that a new spacecraft carried astronauts to space on its very first mission. (Usually, a new spacecraft would be tested first without people on board.) That's how confident NASA was in its new machine.

And like the Apollo program before it, the space shuttle became a source of national pride. When *Columbia* landed at Edwards Air Force Base in the California desert on April 14, 1981, after orbiting the earth thirty-six times, about 225,000 people gathered to witness the historic moment. Like John Glenn had been back in 1962, the astronauts were hailed as heroes and honored with parades.

WHAT IS A VACUUM?

When you hear the word VACUUM, you might think of the common household appliance that we use to remove dirt and debris from carpets. But in science, a vacuum refers to space that has no matter—no solids, liquids, or air.

Scientists don't really know if such a thing as a perfect vacuum exists, because removing all particles of matter from a particular space is extremely difficult. Outer space is considered a nearly perfect vacuum because of how little matter it holds.

While she continued to play the flute with the Stanford Symphony Orchestra (and was recognized for her solo performances), she was also studying electrical engineering—the field she had been discouraged from pursuing as an undergraduate because she was a woman. Ellen learned about the new opportunities at NASA from her classmates at Stanford. "Some of them were saying, 'We're sending in applications,'" she recalled years later in an interview with the *Harvard Gazette*. "And I remembered thinking, 'Really, you can just send in your application?'"

The space shuttle was intended in part to serve as a laboratory where scientists could conduct experiments that were not possible on Earth due to the effects of gravity. For Ellen, this was an exciting development because it created opportunities for research that had never been done before. She herself was becoming a researcher and, as she said on the San Diego State University podcast *Fireside Charla* in April 2020, she was thrilled by "the thought of being able to do research in a unique laboratory, experiments you couldn't do anywhere else, because either you were in a microgravity environment, or you were above the earth's atmosphere, or you had access to almost a complete vacuum."

In 1983, while Ellen was working on her PhD at Stanford, the United States reached another milestone in its space-exploration program. That year, Sally Ride became the first American woman in space as part of a mission on the space shuttle *Challenger*. Ellen and Sally had a few things in common. Sally was born in Los Angeles and had graduated from Stanford University, where Ellen was studying. And just like Ellen, she majored in physics in college.

Seeing a female scientist like Sally Ride travel to space was a huge moment for Ellen; it gave her permission to dream that one day she, too, could become an astronaut. "That was really the first inkling in my brain of, 'Wow, you can get a PhD, you can be headed on a research career, and you could actually do research in space if you got selected,'" Ellen later said on Tufts University's *Tell Me More* podcast.

Around the time that NASA started to hire female astronauts, they began recruiting more members of various minority groups. In 1986, three years after Sally Ride made history, Franklin Chang-Díaz, who was born in Costa Rica, became the first Hispanic person selected by NASA for its astronaut program. The first person from Latin America to go to space was Arnaldo Tamayo Méndez, from Cuba, who in 1980 was part of the Soviet

THE FIRST HISPANIC NASA ASTRONAUT

FRANKLIN CHANG-DÍAZ was born in Costa Rica in 1950 to Ramón A. Chang-Morales (who had Chinese roots) and María Eugenia Díaz De Chang. Growing up during the early days of space exploration, Franklin was absolutely fascinated by the field. As a kid, he and his cousins would pretend that a cardboard box was a spaceship, blasting off from Earth and into the heavens.

Determined to become an astronaut, Franklin finished high school in Costa Rica, then moved to the United States. Because he spoke only Spanish at the time, however, he was forced to complete high school again in the United States. This was difficult, but Franklin's determination eventually paid off, and he was admitted to the University of Connecticut. There he earned a degree in mechanical engineering, and then he went on to study physics and nuclear energy at the Massachusetts Institute of Technology in Boston.

When Franklin was accepted to NASA's space program in 1977, he realized his dream of becoming an astronaut. He traveled to space for the first time in 1986, aboard the space shuttle *Columbia*. By the time he retired from NASA in 2005, Franklin was part of a total of seven space shuttle missions and had participated in three spacewalks (which is when astronauts exit the aircraft in space to perform repairs or install equipment, a very risky activity!).

Union's Soyuz 38 mission. Tamayo was also the first Black person in space.

As with Sally Ride, Chang-Díaz's accomplishment was another inspiring moment for Ellen. "Things were changing. Certainly, the space world was changing," she told CNBC. "I really needed to see those kinds of comparisons for me to think about it."

It would take her more time to receive the opportunity to fulfill her dream, but while a student at Stanford, Ellen was already showing the kinds of skills that one day would get NASA's attention. She was helping to create and design systems that would make it easier to understand and study objects in space through images taken from Earth or satellites. At that point, Ellen intended to finish her PhD and apply to NASA upon her graduation. As part of her plan, she had written to the agency to get more information about what they were looking for in astronaut candidates. "It seemed like the perfect marriage of interest in space and really being able to do exciting research," Ellen told ABC News regarding her goal of becoming an astronaut.

At the same time, Ellen recognized that being selected was a long shot. NASA would only choose a handful of people from thousands of applicants. "Knowing how many people actually apply, I never expected to hear anything back from NASA," she said on the *Wisdom from the Top with Guy Raz* podcast. "I had looked for and interviewed for other jobs for PhD researchers."

CHAPTER THREE

A SCIENTIST IN ACTION

"What I really hope for young people is that they find a career they're passionate about, something that's challenging and worthwhile."

—ELLEN OCHOA

Even before she herself became an astronaut, Ellen was working to help other scientists understand outer space better. In 1985, after finishing her PhD at Stanford and officially becoming Dr. Ellen Ochoa, she continued her research on optical systems at the Sandia National Laboratories, a US government facility in Albuquerque, New Mexico. There she developed two inventions that would also be patented.

Then, as she had planned, Ellen applied to become an astronaut.

WHAT ARE
ELLEN OCHOA'S PATENTS?

When people invent things, they often seek legal documents from the government called PATENTS. Patents serve as proof of ownership, which gives inventors the right to stop other people from duplicating or selling their inventions for a certain number of years. Patents are a way to protect ideas and make sure that only the inventors can make money or receive credit for their innovations.

In addition to being an astronaut, Ellen Ochoa is also an inventor, and she is listed as a coinventor on three different patented technologies. The first, which she helped develop while she was a graduate student at Stanford University, is a device that looks for errors in repeating patterns in order to find defects on an object.

Later, when she worked at Sandia National Laboratories, Ellen and her colleagues designed another optical system that makes it possible for a computer to find a particular object within an image.

Her third patent is for a system that reduces distortions in images, which is known as "noise" in optics. All these inventions helped scientists find small but significant details in images taken from space as well as on Earth.

Six months after she submitted her application, how-ever, a tragedy put NASA's astronaut program on hold. On January 28, 1986, the space shuttle *Challenger*—the same spacecraft that had originally taken Ellen's idol, Sally Ride, to space years earlier—exploded just seventy-three seconds after it took off from the Kennedy Space Center in Cape Canaveral, Florida. None of the seven astronauts on the shuttle survived. Among those killed were Ronald McNair, Ellison S. Onizuka, and Judith Resnik—three of the astronauts who had made the 1978 NASA class the most diverse ever.

This was not the first time that US astronauts had lost their lives on the job. In 1967, during the Apollo program, a fire resulted in the deaths of three crew members during a launch rehearsal. But that accident had occurred on the ground. The *Challenger* disas-ter marked the first time a fatal accident occurred on an American spacecraft *during flight*. Many people, including family members of the astronauts who were killed, had traveled to Cape Canaveral for the launch and saw *Challenger* explode with their own eyes. Mil-lions more witnessed the heart-wrenching events live on television. It was a devastating moment for the country.

THE TEACHER
ABOARD *CHALLENGER*

To receive money from the government for its work, NASA needed public support. Public interest in the space shuttle program, however, was waning. To regain the excitement of average Americans about spaceflight, the agency decided to send a civilian into space. Among those killed in the 1986 Challenger accident was CHRISTA McAULIFFE, a thirty-seven-year-old social studies teacher from New Hampshire.

Christa became the first civilian to go to space as part of the Teacher in Space Project, which President Ronald Reagan announced in 1984. Approximately eleven thousand teachers from across the country applied, and NASA selected Christa and her backup, Barbara Radding Morgan. The two teachers trained for 114 hours alongside astronauts for the mission.

After the *Challenger* tragedy, however, plans to send more civilians in space were halted. More than two decades later, in 2007, Barbara became the first teacher to visit space as part of mission STS-118, flown on the space shuttle *Endeavor*, which NASA built to replace *Challenger*.

President Ronald Reagan addressed the nation on television after the *Challenger* tragedy and ordered an investigation to figure out what had gone wrong. It determined that the space shuttle had exploded because of a problem with a rubber seal on one of the rocket boosters, known as an O-ring. The purpose of these rubber seals was to prevent the hot gases inside the rocket boosters from escaping. The O-rings were sensitive to the cold, and temperatures were below freezing in Florida the day of the launch. As a result, an O-ring on one of the rocket boosters attached to the *Challenger* orbiter did not expand as it should have. Because the O-ring did not work properly, gases leaked out, and a hydrogen fuel tank caught fire, leading to the explosion.

The investigation also discovered that some engineers who worked for the company that made the rocket boosters had tried to warn NASA leadership that the O-rings would not perform as they should in cold temperatures, leading to a catastrophic explosion. They thought the *Challenger* launch should be postponed until the problem was resolved. But NASA officials had dismissed their concerns and warnings. That meant it wasn't just the O-rings themselves that NASA had to fix; to avoid more disasters, the agency had to work on creating a culture in which all expert opinions and concerns about safety were taken seriously.

As a result, it would be more than two years before NASA attempted to fly another space shuttle. In the meantime, the agency began building a new shuttle, called *Endeavor*, to take *Challenger*'s place in the fleet. While the *Challenger* tragedy did not mark the end of the space shuttle program, it reminded everyone that these spacecraft were imperfect machines and space exploration can be dangerous—and sometimes deadly—work.

Naturally, Ellen questioned her desire to become an astronaut after the *Challenger* accident. "I think if you are not a little scared, you don't understand the risks," she would later say about spaceflight in an interview with the *Los Angeles Times*. But despite the risks, she decided that going to space was still a dream that was worth pursuing.

WHY EXPLORE SPACE?

Exploring outer space requires substantial time and money. And as past accidents have shown us, it can be dangerous work that has cost people their lives.

So, why do countries take such great risks to explore space?

Natural human curiosity surely plays a role. By exploring space, we can learn more about the origins of the universe, the solar system, and our place within the cosmos. This can help us understand some big mysteries, like whether there is life beyond Earth.

But there are other potential benefits to space exploration. For example, research done in space allows scientists to better understand Earth's environment and helps people on the ground adjust to changes in climate. One day, scientists hope to land humans on asteroids—rocks smaller than a planet that orbit the sun—in order to learn more about them and to be better prepared to take action in case one were to collide with Earth again. (An asteroid collision is believed to have wiped out the dinosaurs around sixty-six million years ago.)

Space also holds great promise for medicine. To keep astronauts healthy in microgravity, experiments and studies conducted in a space laboratory, the International Space Station, have led to new ways to diagnose and treat medical conditions. For example, NASA has invented methods for looking inside the human body and performing surgery. And when we are sick, our bodies produce certain substances. These substances behave differently with and without gravity. By running experiments without gravity, scientists can potentially develop treatments for cancer and other illnesses that they might not be able to create under Earth's gravitational pull.

In 1987, almost two years after she submitted her first application, Ellen got exciting news—she was a finalist for NASA's astronaut program! As a finalist, she got to spend an entire week at the Johnson Space Center in Houston, which was a thrilling experience in and of itself. "I was pretty excited to have already made it that far in the process," Ellen later said in a December 2021 podcast interview.

At the Johnson Space Center, Ellen met and spoke to astronauts for the first time and found out more about what the job involved. She also took many medical tests to make sure that she was mentally and physically healthy enough to undergo rigorous astronaut training and eventually travel to space.

Unfortunately, Ellen was not accepted into the astronaut program at that moment. However, she had impressed enough people at NASA that they encouraged her to keep her application active and updated for future consideration.

"I couldn't say I was expecting to be selected. So many people apply and so few are chosen that I didn't see it as a failure because the odds seemed too great to begin with," Ellen later said on *Wisdom from the Top*. "In fact, I kind of viewed myself as 'I'm a long shot. I seem so different from most people you think of as astronauts,' although I would try to keep in mind people like Sally Ride and others who at least had some things in common with me. So, as disappointed as I was, I can't say that I felt like I had failed."

But despite her disappointment and the extremely low chances of being chosen, Ellen's visit to the Johnson Space Center left her more driven than ever to become an astronaut. During her time there, she realized that most people who were hired as astronauts had a pilot's license, since operating a spacecraft is in many ways like flying an airplane. Both require operators to make split-second decisions while under pressure. "If you go out and get a private pilot's license, now you are learning to operate in an environment that is a lot similar to what an astronaut would do," Ellen said.

As a researcher, Ellen had spent much time conducting experiments in labs and writing scientific papers to explain her findings. By learning to fly a plane, she could show NASA that she had the skills to work inside a spacecraft, too. After the agency rejected her first application for the astronaut program, Ellen took flying lessons at the airport near her home in California and became a private pilot to improve her chances of getting selected in the future.

Her visit to Johnson Space Center also made Ellen realize that she wanted to work for NASA and be involved in space exploration one way or another. "I had been so excited about actually being at Johnson Center, which just seemed like the most amazing place where all these human spaceflight milestones had happened," Ellen said on *Wisdom from the Top*. Whether or not she became an astronaut, she wanted to be a part of this incredible effort.

So, even as she worked to become a stronger candidate for the astronaut program, Ellen applied for and received another position as a research engineer at Ames Research Center, a NASA facility in California that conducts research to support spaceflight and space exploration. Some discoveries and technologies made at Ames had been crucial to the Apollo lunar missions, as well as to the space shuttle program. At Ames, Ellen was soon promoted to lead a group of about thirty-five engineers who were working to develop computer systems to be used in space. Women—especially women of color—were rarely given opportunities to become leaders, so this was another huge accomplishment for Ellen.

While working at the Ames Research Center, Ellen kept her application for the astronaut program active and updated, just like she had been advised to do. Then one day, in January 1990, she received a phone call at work from Donald Puddy, the director of flight crew operations at the Johnson Space Center. Knowing that Donald would be the person making the call if she were selected for the astronaut program, Ellen realized she finally had succeeded in becoming an astronaut. "You never forget that moment. It was probably the most amazing moment of my life," Ellen later said on *Wisdom from the Top*. "I knew my life would change forever."

On January 17, 1990, Ellen was announced as a member of NASA Astronaut Group 13, which included twenty-three astronauts selected from a pool of around two thousand applicants. Meanwhile, Ellen was only one of five women in her group. She was accepted to the program as a mission specialist, an astronaut who focuses on specific tasks or experiments while the crew is in space. Ellen's group called itself "the Hairballs"—a reference to black cats, which, like the number thirteen, were considered unlucky.

Despite working so hard to get that far in her career as

a scientist, Ellen sometimes would hear disparaging comments from people who questioned if women could really handle such a difficult job. "Looking back, every time somebody told me that I couldn't do something or it probably wasn't suited for me, or made some comment about women or other underrepresented groups, they were really just revealing [their own] bias," Ellen told CNBC.

Since she had made history as the first Latina astronaut, Ellen suddenly found herself in the spotlight. Schools all over the country, including many with large numbers of Hispanic students, asked Ellen to visit their classrooms to talk about her career. They knew she would be an inspiration to those children.

CHAPTER FOUR

A HISTORIC MISSION TO SPACE

"I can only imagine the amazement and pride that my grandparents would feel . . . knowing that their granddaughter grew up to, not only to travel to space, but to have their name and their heritage used to inspire future generations."

—Ellen Ochoa

Once she was accepted into NASA's astronaut program, Ellen came one step closer to her dream of going to space—something no woman of Hispanic descent had ever done. It would be a while, however, before that happened. First, Ellen had to complete intensive training to know how to live and work in an environment that is quite different from Earth. Astronauts typically train for about two years before they can go to space.

Before she reported for training, Ellen married her boyfriend, Coe Miles, who she had met while working at the Ames Research Center. When they met, Coe was a scientist, working for the center as a contractor. Ellen and Coe moved to Houston, where Ellen would train at the Johnson Space Center.

Ellen and the other members of NASA Astronaut Group 13 began their training in July 1990. Astronauts have a lot to learn before they are prepared to go into space—how their spacecraft works, how to operate the equipment needed to perform experiments, and how to take care of their bodies and minds in such a drastically different environment. This required them to learn new sleeping habits, change the way they ate, and make other challenging adjustments to the way they ordinarily lived.

As part of their training, astronauts use simulators to get a sense of what it's like to launch into space and then land on Earth. In space if something malfunctions or someone has a medical emergency, there is no one to come to the rescue. Therefore, astronauts need training on how to fix any problems on their own, even with guidance from the ground.

In Ellen's words, astronaut training was "a lot like school." But in addition to reading books, completing assignments and listening to experts' lectures, Ellen also did things she never had before. For example, she had to fly in a high-performance jet plane and learn how to eject, or exit, safely out of an aircraft. She practiced landing in the ocean with the help of a parachute, climbing onto a raft, then getting picked up by a helicopter.

To understand what it feels like to perform a spacewalk,

Ellen scuba dived in a giant pool. "Those were things that were pretty far outside of my experience, not to mention comfort zone," Ellen would later say on the SDSU *Fireside Charla* podcast, jokingly noting that she had never even been a Girl Scout as a kid.

Ellen had to learn how all the systems in the space shuttle *Discovery* worked and what steps to take if something unexpected happened—for example, if the space shuttle lost contact with NASA on the ground. "You spend just a little bit of time going through the procedures as they're written, and then you spend most of the rest of the training period trying to figure out how you will work around problems that you have," Ellen said when describing her astronaut training.

Because she had been admitted to the astronaut program as a mission specialist, Ellen trained to work the Remote Manipulator System—a robotic arm attached to the space shuttle that crews used to release and retrieve scientific instruments from space. Like a human arm, the robotic arm had multiple joints, like our elbows, as well as a claw at the end that can grab objects. However, at fifty feet long, it was *much* longer than a human arm, and according to Smithsonian Education, Ellen has compared using the robotic arm to playing a video game.

After finishing her second year of training, Ellen received more life-changing news: She was one of five astronauts assigned to mission STS-56, aboard the space shuttle *Discovery*. The countdown to becoming the first Latina in space had begun.

It was extremely dark out when Ellen and the other four astronauts assigned to mission STS-56 made their way to the space shuttle *Discovery* at Florida's Kennedy Space Center in the early hours of April 8, 1993.

This would be their second attempt at launch. Two days earlier, Ellen and her crewmates had been in the shuttle, ready to go, when computers detected a problem with the orbiter's propulsion system—the part of a spacecraft that pushes it upward and allows it to escape Earth's gravitational pull. With just eleven seconds remaining before takeoff, the computers had automatically stopped the countdown to launch, as they had been programmed to do.

NASA had to delay the launch because a problem with the propulsion system could lead to a fuel leak and cause a deadly explosion, as had happened with *Challenger*. The agency's scientists needed to make sure everything was working properly before they could try again. In the end, it turned out that the propulsion system was just fine. The glitch had been with the computers themselves.

As the astronauts drove out to the launchpad on April 8, one of the few things Ellen could see in the darkness was the huge bright xenon lights that illuminated the shuttle. Soon she found herself in the elevator that would take her to the entrance of the crew cabin, which is 195 feet above the ground. "It feels like it's alive. It's kind of hissing, and you see a little bit of fog here and there coming out of different places on the shuttle," Ellen later said on the *Wisdom from the Top* podcast.

At 1:29 a.m. EST, with all the astronauts strapped in their seats, *Discovery* took off from launchpad 39B, traveling at a speed of about 17,500 miles per hour. For the first two minutes, according to the *Los Angeles Times*, Ellen saw a lot of light and felt "a lot of rumbling and vibration." The ride got smoother from there as the rocket boosters separated and fell back to Earth as they were designed to do. When *Discovery* went into orbit around the planet eight and a half minutes after takeoff, Ellen made history: She was, officially, the first Hispanic woman in space.

As with previous space shuttle missions, the astronauts on STS-56 were expected to conduct experiments. The purpose of the STS-56 mission was to learn more about the ozone layer—the layer of Earth's atmosphere that absorbs most of the harmful ultraviolet light released by the sun. "It was something I was very excited

to participate in, and I loved working with the team and with my crew and doing work that was important to understanding changes in the atmosphere," Ellen said in an interview with the *TODAY* show.

WHY IS THE OZONE LAYER IMPORTANT?

OZONE is a gas that absorbs harmful ultraviolet light from the sun. Located about fifteen miles above the surface of Earth in a part of the atmosphere known as the stratosphere, the ozone layer stops ultraviolet light rays from reaching us. Excessive exposure to this radiation can cause skin cancer (which is why we wear sunscreen) and cataracts, which is a clouding of the lens in our eyes that can make things look blurry or, in severe cases, lead to blindness.

But over time human activity has caused severe damage to the ozone layer. Human-made chemicals known as chlorofluorocarbons (CFCs), for example, which are used in aerosol sprays and cooling appliances like refrigerators and air conditioners, break up the ozone layer when they are released into the atmosphere. The first scientist to realize the effect of CFCs on the ozone layer was Mario

Molina, who was from Mexico, just like Ellen's grandparents.

Because of their excessive use, CFCs were destroying the ozone in the stratosphere faster than it could replenish itself, causing the layer that sits over the South Pole to become thinner. Scientists first detected this "hole" in the ozone layer in the 1970s and 1980s. As a result of their discovery—and the warnings they issued—in 1987, every country signed an international agreement known as the Montreal Protocol, which banned the use of CFCs. The ban has allowed the ozone layer to repair itself. Over time, the hole has shrunk, and it is expected to be completely repaired by the year 2070.

As part of this mission, the crew would release a scientific satellite to observe and study the sun's atmosphere, called the corona, as well as the electrically charged particles that the corona releases, known as solar wind. Such experiments could not be conducted on Earth and could be valuable in understanding the damage that had been done to the ozone layer.

One of Ellen's most important jobs on STS-56 was to

use the *Discovery*'s robotic arm to release and retrieve the satellite—a complicated process. "The only thing I [was] really nervous about for the whole mission was, 'Am I going to do everything right?'" said Ellen on the *Stanford Pathfinders* podcast. "If I screw that up, we've lost that whole science satellite part of the mission. So, you're just really focused on trying to think through all of your training."

Everything went as planned. Despite being nervous, Ellen's NASA training and her knowledge of math and physics enabled her to successfully maneuver the experiment properly. She used the robotic arm to release the

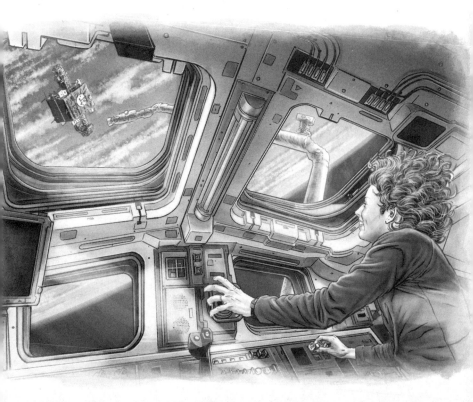

2,800-pound satellite on April 11, just as *Discovery* was flying over Greece, and retrieved it on April 13.

"Great work," fellow astronaut Kevin Chilton told Ellen from mission control—the group of people who direct spaceflights from Earth—back in Houston. "There are a lot of smiles in the room down here."

"She did it very carefully, very slowly, very methodically, with extreme concentration . . . and it was a gem," fellow Mexican American Earl Montoya, the program manager on the ground at NASA who was responsible for designing and operating the experiment, told the *Los Angeles Times*.

For her first trip into outer space, Ellen had packed a special personal possession—the flute she'd owned since she was a senior in high school. Although she was now a scientist, her love of music had never left her. At that time, musical instruments were rarely allowed on space shuttle missions, largely because of safety concerns. Some instruments and even the cases they are carried in can emit radiation that can interfere with the electrical systems inside the shuttle. Other instruments can also release gases that can endanger the crew. Wooden instruments like a guitar can catch flames. Sometimes changes can be made to the instruments so that it is safe to take them on the space shuttle, and the astronauts must be careful to properly store the instruments when they aren't playing.

Fortunately for Ellen, the astronauts on STS-56 were planning to film a video for children during their mission about what it's like to live in space. Therefore, she was able to convince her superiors to let her bring a flute on board. On shuttle missions like STS-56, which only lasted a few days, the scientists did not have a lot of time for hobbies or other fun activities. But for fifteen minutes, Ellen serenaded the rest of the crew with her flute.

STS-56 lasted nine days. During the mission, Ellen and the other astronauts on the space shuttle *Discovery* communicated with schools down on Earth via radio. They also contacted the Russian space station Mir, which showed how much space exploration had changed since the Cold War. Even though she was busy, Ellen made sure to take in the experience of being in space, something that few humans get to do. "I must say it's a bit hard to keep my concentration because [I'm] looking out the window at some great views of South America right now," Ellen joked at one point while she spoke with mission control, as seen on a NASA video from that mission.

Ellen and her fellow astronauts returned home on April 17, 1993, landing at Kennedy Space Center at 7:37 a.m. EST. By then, space shuttle flights had become more common and drew less attention. But as the first Latina astronaut, Ellen was flooded with requests to visit schools. She quickly realized just how much her achievement meant to the Hispanic community and how much of a role model she could be for others, like Sally Ride and Franklin Chang-Díaz had been for her.

"It was eye-opening," Ellen said in a 2021 interview with the *TODAY* show. "Everybody is out there cheering and greeting me in a way I hadn't seen before. I realized, 'This is bigger than I was originally thinking.'"

LATINX MILESTONES IN SPACE

Ellen Ochoa (Mexico): First Latina in space

Arnaldo Tamayo Méndez (Cuba): First Latin American, first person of African descent, and first Cuban to fly in space

Franklin Chang-Díaz (Costa Rica): First Latin American NASA astronaut to travel to space

Rodolfo Neri Vela (Mexico): Second Latin American NASA astronaut to travel to space

Joseph Michael "Joe" Acaba (Puerto Rico): First NASA astronaut of Puerto Rican descent

John Daniel "Danny" Olivas (Mexico): First person of Mexican American heritage to walk in space

Ellen's work contributed to the success of STS-56, and she was just getting started as an astronaut. She returned to space in November 1994, this time aboard the space shuttle *Atlantis*, for mission STS-66. As with Ellen's first mission, the purpose of this flight was to gather more information about the effect of the sun on the ozone layer. Once again, Ellen's job was to operate the space shuttle's robotic arm to perform the tricky maneuver of releasing and then retrieving a satellite.

With one mission under her belt, she was as successful in her role as she had been the first time. Back on Earth, at the Kennedy Space Center, scientists shouted "Super! Super!" as Ellen retrieved the satellite. They celebrated with gummy bears.

With her first two assignments, Ellen had fulfilled the ambition that had led her to NASA—to conduct experiments in space. "My first two missions were really kind of exactly what I was thinking about when I first thought about wanting to be an astronaut and applying for the program," Ellen later said on SDSU's *Fireside Charla*. "It was an opportunity to do research in space that couldn't be done on the ground."

CHAPTER FIVE

BUILDING THE INTERNATIONAL SPACE STATION

"I felt like I was contributing to something larger than myself, that benefits people on Earth."

—ELLEN OCHOA, *Harvard Gazette*

NASA's space shuttle program ran from 1981 to 2011, and one of its most important accomplishments was building the enormous space laboratory known as the International Space Station (ISS). As you might figure out from its name, the ISS is a joint effort among several countries. Those countries include the United States and Russia, formerly the Soviet Union, which collapsed in 1991. Though the United States had competed against the Soviet Union during the Space Race, after the Cold War, the United States and Russia decided to work together on space exploration. And the result was marvelous.

President Ronald Reagan had ordered the construction of the ISS in 1984, while Ellen was still a graduate student at Stanford University. When she first heard of the plans to build the space station, she probably had no idea that one day she would play a role in building this massive laboratory. Russia launched the first piece of the ISS called the *Zarya Module* in 1998. A month later, the United States contributed its first piece of the ISS—the *Unity Module*, which was launched and attached to the *Zarya Module*.

The next phase of the project was to prepare the station for people to live in it. One of Ellen's responsibilities at NASA would be working with Russia's space agency, Roskosmos, to decide how to select crews headed for the ISS and determine how they would overcome language barriers. "It was an incredibly interesting time and something I had really never thought about being a part of earlier on when I was interested in the astronaut program," Ellen later said on SDSU's *Fireside Charla*. In 1999, Ellen was assigned to her third space shuttle mission, STS-96, aboard the space shuttle *Discovery*. This mission was NASA's first attempt to dock, or connect to, the ISS.

The goal of STS-96 was to deliver four tons of equipment and supplies—like laptops, water, sleeping bags, trash bags, clothing, and medical equipment—to the ISS for the astronauts who later would live there full-time. Ellen oversaw the transfer of everything from the *Discovery* to the ISS, handing off each suitcase, one by one, to her fellow crew members.

Ellen's personal life had changed a lot since she'd last traveled to space six years earlier. She was now the mom of a one-year-old boy named Wilson. Astronauts must spend a week in isolation before going to space to make sure they do not catch any diseases prior to their mission. Being in Florida for almost three weeks to prepare for STS-96 meant that Ellen would miss Wilson's first birthday. Those are the kinds of sacrifices an astronaut or other people in demanding jobs must often make. Knowing that her son would miss her while she was away on her mission, Ellen recorded a video of herself with Wilson so that he could watch it while she was in space.

WHAT IS THE INTERNATIONAL SPACE STATION?

Roughly the size of a football field, the International Space Station (ISS) is the largest human-made object ever launched into space to date. Weighing close to a million pounds, it orbits the earth at 250 miles above the surface and travels at a speed of almost five miles per second. This means it circles the planet sixteen times in a single day.

The ISS was built by the space agencies of the United States, Russia, Canada, Japan, as well as the European Space Agency, which represents twenty-two European countries. The first part of the ISS, the *Zarya Module*, was launched on November 20, 1998, and the first crew arrived at the ISS on November 2, 2000. After thirteen years and forty missions, the ISS was completed in 2011. It has a total of sixteen modules: six launched by Russia, eight launched by the United States, and one each from Japan and the European Space Agency.

Since 2000, the ISS has been occupied continuously by people. Six astronauts can live inside the ISS at one time. It has two bathrooms, a gymnasium (in space, astronauts must exercise for several hours a day to prevent bone and muscle loss caused by the lack of gravity), and six sleeping rooms. The ISS also serves as a science laboratory, where astronauts conduct experiments in an environment unaffected by Earth's gravity.

Although the length of their stay depends on what kind of work they are doing, astronauts usually are assigned to the ISS for six months at a time. Because they are up there for such long stretches, astronauts on the ISS have time off to relax and pursue personal activities—like playing instruments.

Like she had done on her first flight, Ellen packed a special object on her first trip to the ISS. Instead of her flute, she brought the gold, white, and purple flag of the National Woman's Party, an organization that was considered instrumental in securing the right to vote for women in the early 1900s. Ellen and the other two female astronauts aboard STS-96, Julie Payette and Tamara Jernigan, took a photo together in which they appear floating inside the space shuttle while holding the flag. In a video for the National Women's History Museum, Ellen said it was her way of "illustrating how far women had come in that time, particularly in the science and engineering fields, and how important voting was to that progress."

During STS-96, which lasted almost ten days, Ellen again worked the shuttle's robotic arm. In addition to supplies, *Discovery* carried a pair of special cranes that would be attached to the ISS so that the station could be expanded in the future. Ellen used the robotic arm to help Jernigan and another astronaut, Daniel Barry, as they conducted an eight-hour spacewalk to attach the two cranes to the ISS. That kind of collaboration gave her great satisfaction.

"Working so closely with a team to accomplish a challenging, meaningful task is the greatest reward of being an astronaut," Ellen would later say to *The Science Teacher* journal.

Ellen's final trip to space, Mission STS-110, occurred in 2002, nine years after her first trip to space. The space shuttle *Atlantis* departed from the Kennedy Space Center in Florida on April 8, 2002. Once again, Ellen's destination was the ISS. The purpose of this mission was to attach a structure made of aluminum and steel known as the S0 truss onto the ISS. The device became the backbone of the ISS so that later it could be expanded. Ellen used the robotic arm to lift the S0 truss out of *Atlantis* and attach it to the Destiny laboratory. With a beam that was forty-four feet long and weighed twenty-seven thousand pounds, this was no easy job, but all went smoothly.

HOW DO ASTRONAUTS COMMUNICATE WITH THEIR FAMILIES?

Even while they are in space, astronauts stay in touch with family back home. During Ellen's first space shuttle flights, she communicated with her husband, Coe, and relatives via email. On her last flight, in 2002, when *Atlantis* docked at the ISS, she was able to dial a phone number from space for the first time and speak with her two young sons. Thanks to more advanced technology, astronauts on the ISS today can arrange video calls with their families.

By then, Ellen had a second son named Jordan. Understanding that she was taking a major risk every time she went to space, Ellen realized that if something went wrong, her two sons would be left without a mother. Yet she believed her work was important enough to justify the risk and had faith that her sons would grow up to feel the same way she did. "If it's something that's really important to you, and in the end you're doing something that's bigger than yourself and that brings benefits to people on Earth,

I think that's the kind of thing that we should be doing. And hopefully, if anything happened, my kids would one day understand why it was so important to me," Ellen later said on the Flute Center of New York's *Flute Unscripted* podcast.

After ten days in space, Mission STS-110 ended, and the space shuttle *Atlantis* returned to Earth. Once the shuttle undocked from the ISS for the return trip, Ellen and the rest of the crew caught a glimpse of "green strands and red filaments"—the aurora australis, or southern lights. "This beautiful, eerie sight mesmerized the crew," Ellen told *The Science Teacher* journal. "Suddenly it was sunrise and the whole station turned a brilliant white and gold, as if a cloaking device had just been removed."

By that point, Ellen had spent 978 hours in space! Yet the sighting of the aurora australis she would remember forever. "I never in my life thought I'd be in the position to see that, to be part of this amazing endeavor," she later said in a speech at a University of Nebraska-Lincoln event.

Her space adventures may have been over, but Ellen would remain an important member of NASA for a long time.

FROM FARMWORKER
TO ASTRONAUT

Fourteen years after Ellen Ochoa's first trip to space, the Space Shuttle *Discovery* once again took off for the International Space Station in 2009. Aboard was California native José M. Hernández, a former farmworker who had spent much of his childhood in agricultural fields, caring for and harvesting crops alongside his Mexican immigrant parents. Teenage José was working in a field near Stockton, California, listening to his radio when he heard that Franklin Chang-Díaz had become the first Latino accepted into NASA's astronaut program.

"That was the moment I said, 'I want to fly in space,'" José says on the José M. Hernández Reaching for the Stars Foundation website.

After high school, José went on to earn degrees in electrical engineering from the University of the Pacific in Stockton and the University of California, Santa Barbara. After years of applying for the astronaut program, he was offered a different job at NASA in 2001.

Although he accepted the job, José continued to aim for the astronaut program. He had been rejected eleven times before he was finally selected for the astronaut program in 2004. José completed astronaut training in 2006 and, along the way, got to meet his hero—Franklin Chang-Díaz.

"It was a strange place to find myself, being evaluated by the person who gave me the motivation to get there in the first place," José says about meeting Franklin. "But I found that we actually had common experiences—a similar upbringing, the same language issues. That built up my confidence. Any barriers that existed, he had already hurdled them."

In 2009 José was a mission specialist aboard STS-128, which docked at the International Space Station to drop off one astronaut and pick up another. Also on that mission was astronaut John "Danny" Olivas, who had become the first man of Mexican descent born in the United States to travel to space two years earlier.

"¡Espero [que] la cosecha de mi sueño sirva como inspiración a todos!" José tweeted from space, in Spanish, his first language. It translates to "I hope the harvest of my dream serves as inspiration to all!"

CHAPTER SIX

LEADING NASA IN A TIME OF TRANSITION

"Being involved in human spaceflight, it is an emotional endeavor. I think it brings in the highest highs and the lowest lows."

—ELLEN OCHOA, NPR

After her final mission, Ellen continued to be deeply involved with human spaceflight. In 2002 she took a new position with NASA as deputy director of Flight Crew Operations at Johnson Space Center. In that role, she helped to oversee the training of other astronauts and worked to make sure that the spacecraft operated during missions according to plan. It was an important job, and because of it, Ellen found herself in mission control on one of the worst days in NASA's history.

After spending two weeks in space on a mission devoted entirely to scientific experiments, the space shuttle *Columbia* was set to return to Earth on February 1, 2003. As it reentered Earth's atmosphere at about 9:00 a.m. EST, however, the spacecraft broke into tens of thousands of pieces as it passed over eastern Texas. None of the seven astronauts on board survived. Ellen was captured on video the moment NASA flight director LeRoy E. Cain conveyed to her the severity of the accident. She is seen briefly shutting her eyes and mouthing two words: "Oh God."

For Ellen, it was both a personal and professional tragedy; she knew all the astronauts who died that day. One of them was Kalpana Chawla, who in 1997 had become the first woman of Indian descent to go to space. Also on the mission was Richard Douglas Husband, who had been the pilot on Ellen's third spaceflight, STS-96, in 1999. Ellen not only knew Husband but his family as well.

Once it became clear that *Columbia* had been lost, Ellen and everyone else in mission control had to follow a series of steps designed to preserve as much information as possible about the accident to discover what went wrong. Ellen was one of the members of NASA who communicated with the astronauts who were living on the

ISS and therefore had to break the tragic news to them. "I've been really fortunate to have had all these amazing moments, but, obviously, *Columbia* was the most difficult thing we had to face at NASA," Ellen later said.

After the *Columbia* accident, NASA shut down the shuttle program again, until 2005. It launched an investigation to determine why the accident had occurred and what could be done to prevent another tragedy in the future. NASA already had an idea of what had gone wrong; video of the launch showed that less than two minutes after *Columbia* took off, a piece of foam had broken off from one of the external fuel tanks and struck the orbiter's left wing.

For years, NASA had known that foam would sometimes come off from the tanks, and some experts in the agency had warned that that could lead to a catastrophic incident. *Columbia* was on its way to space when NASA had realized that foam had broken off and hit the left wing, and staff on the ground tried to figure out how bad the damage was. Some people at NASA suggested that the agency try to get a Department of Defense spy satellite to take pictures of the orbiter to get a better look at the damaged wing, but NASA officials decided against it.

Ultimately, nothing was done to address the problem before the space shuttle tried to return to Earth. It turned out that the foam had damaged the tiles that protected the orbiter from heat. As a result, intense hot winds got inside the orbiter when it reentered Earth's atmosphere, causing the spacecraft to disintegrate. As had been the case with the *Challenger* accident, NASA's failure to fix a known problem led to another tragedy.

"In addition to technical failures, we came to understand that the safety of the [*Columbia*] mission was compromised because the right conversations with the right people never quite happened," Ellen later said in an interview on Stanford University's website.

Eventually, Ellen became director of Flight Crew Operations at Johnson Space Center. In that role, she strived to apply the painful lessons about failed communication and unheeded warnings at NASA that resulted in the *Challenger* and *Columbia* disasters. She ensured that everyone in her division felt comfortable expressing concerns about safety to leadership and that every voice would be heard: "I really did couch it as, 'This is our job. It's not that we want you to speak up. We need you to speak up. And you need to feel that part of your job is speaking up. That's the only way we can prevent another accident,'" she said on *Wisdom from the Top.*

In 2007, five years after her final space shuttle flight, Ellen officially retired as an astronaut. She was not, however, done making history. During her years at NASA, Ellen had impressed her colleagues with not only her skills as a scientist and engineer but also her leadership abilities and her willingness to take on big challenges. In November 2007 she was named deputy director of the Johnson Space Center—a big accomplishment and not her last. In 2012, Ellen broke yet another barrier when she became just the second woman and the first person of Hispanic descent to be named director of the JSC.

Ellen became the leader of Johnson Space Center at a time of transition. The agency was shifting its focus away from the space shuttle program, which ended in July 2011 after 135 missions, to new approaches to exploration. As director, Ellen took the time to meet with a group of JSC employees over coffee once a month to hear what was on their minds; it was her attempt at making sure that everyone who worked there felt they could voice ideas and opinions over how the institution could best achieve its goals.

Under Ellen's leadership, NASA began partnering with private companies to send supplies to the ISS and bring the results of scientific experiments back to Earth. During Ellen's time as director, NASA selected two new astronaut classes, one in 2013 and another in 2017. These astronauts were expected to be part of missions to the ISS. However, they took the job knowing that one day they could be assigned to missions into deep space. But NASA's first goal is to set up a permanent base on the moon. That's an important "stepping stone" toward the next major goal on the list: a human flight to the planet Mars.

GETTING TO KNOW MARS

Known as the Red Planet and named for the Roman god of war, Mars is the fourth planet from the sun. The dust that covers the surface of Mars contains large quantities of rusted iron, which is why the planet looks red to us. Because it is much farther from the sun than Earth is—Mars orbits the sun at an average distance of 142 million miles—it's much colder there than it is on Earth; temperatures there can fall to -81 degrees Fahrenheit.

Mars takes 687 days to orbit the sun. That means that a year on Mars is almost twice as long as a year on Earth. However, a day on Mars is about the same length as a day on Earth—just about forty minutes longer. With a radius of 2,106 miles, Mars is roughly half the size of Earth. That means there's a lot less gravity on Mars, and we all would weigh less there. Mars has two moons of its own, named Phobos and Deimos.

One of the most important questions scientists have about Mars is whether the planet ever supported life. For life to have been possible on Mars, there had to have been water. Thanks to fly-by spacecraft that have collected information about the planet and rovers operated from Earth that have landed on its surface, we know that there are many canyons on the surface of Mars. Because canyons on Earth are carved by water, this discovery suggests that water once flowed on Mars, too.

Ice made of frozen water has been discovered below the Martian surface. This is important, because before humans can go to Mars, scientists must figure out how to make sure they will have enough water to survive. In fact, figuring out where the water on Mars is located will help scientists determine where on the planet a human mission could land.

Astronomers also know that Mars has no oxygen, so ensuring that people will be able to breathe there is another challenge. The planet's atmosphere is thin and made of carbon dioxide, so NASA is figuring out how to convert that carbon dioxide to oxygen. And then there's radiation from the sun. On Mars, the thin atmosphere would mean that astronauts would be exposed to a lot more radiation than they are exposed to on Earth, which eventually could cause serious illness. If humans are to survive on Mars, scientists must find a solution for that, too.

The focus on reaching Mars has become a bigger priority for NASA over the years. While Ellen was the director of the Johnson Space Center, the agency started testing parts of *Orion*, a new spacecraft named after the constellation. *Orion* was built with the goal of taking human beings deeper into space than ever before. On December 5, 2014, Ellen watched as a cone-shaped *Orion* spacecraft took off from Kennedy Space Center, like she had on each of her four space shuttle missions.

One aspect of the spacecraft that was tested was a heat shield designed to protect the astronauts inside from temperatures of up to 4,000 degrees Fahrenheit when reentering Earth's atmosphere. The spacecraft traveled thirty-six hundred miles above Earth, farther than any spacecraft had since Apollo 17, the last of the Apollo lunar missions, in 1972. It landed in the Pacific Ocean, six hundred miles off the coast of Ellen's native San Diego, and was recovered by members of NASA and the US Navy.

Even though there were no people on board *Orion*, Ellen was delighted to see the public's excitement over this important milestone in the quest to send humans to Mars. "I was actually really, really happy with how much

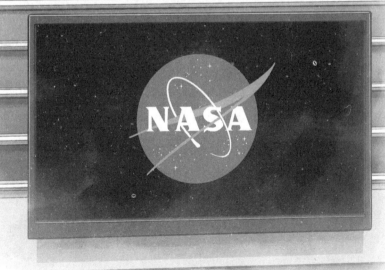

attention it did get from people, not just even around the country but around the world," Ellen told the NASA Johnson Space Center Oral History Project. "It can be a little bit difficult to generate that when there aren't people on board, even though it's a human-rated spacecraft . . . I think we did a really good job of explaining why it was such an important flight for us."

While Ellen was the director, Johnson Space Center also took other steps that scientists hope will advance the goal of a human mission to Mars. Beginning in March 2015, American astronaut Scott Kelly and Russian cosmonaut Mikhail Kornienko spent a year at the International Space Station. Scott and Mikhail stayed twice the length of an astronaut's usual stay to help scientists better understand how living in space affects the human mind and body.

That knowledge is vital preparation for future human voyages to a place like Mars. A one-way trip to the Red Planet is estimated to take at least seven to nine months. That means astronauts who embark on the journey would be away from Earth for about three years. Therefore, scientists must first learn if it's even possible to keep humans safe—mentally and physically—in space for such a long period of time and then help them readjust to gravity when they return to Earth.

The experiment with Scott and Mikhail was a step in that direction. Scott was selected for the yearlong ISS mission because he has an identical twin brother, Mark, who was also an astronaut. Comparing Scott's body to that of his twin after Scott had lived at the ISS for a year made it possible for researchers to learn more about changes that happen to the human body during long periods in space in a state of microgravity.

They learned that during his time in space, Scott's DNA—genetic material found in each of our cells— changed, though most of it went back to normal when he returned to Earth. Still, this is concerning, because changes in DNA can eventually lead to diseases like cancer. There were changes in the bacteria in Scott's gut while he was in space, and his vision got worse. After returning to Earth, his cognitive abilities—things like memory, attention span, and ability to use logic to solve problems—also declined. Along with other studies, these changes Scott experienced will help scientists understand the risks involved with sending humans to Mars and perhaps help them develop ways to reduce them.

In 2018 Ellen retired from NASA after a thirty-year career with the agency. By that point, she had already been inducted into the Astronaut Hall of Fame, which is just one of the many recognitions she earned in her career. She has received the Distinguished Service Medal, which is NASA's highest award, and the Presidential Distinguished Rank Award for her work as a government executive. And there are at least six schools named after her.

"Education was important to my family and key to my career, so to see that, that's something that's going to live on," Ellen told the *TODAY* show.

After Ellen's retirement, she and her husband, Coe, moved to Boise, Idaho, where she bought a new flute and started taking lessons again. But even after leaving NASA, Ellen has remained involved in the scientific community. She went on to serve as chair of the National Science Board, which is a group of experts that oversees the National Science Foundation and helps the president and Congress make decisions when it comes to funding scientific research.

Always aware that she has become a role model for other women, especially other Latinas, Ellen continues to give talks and presentations about her experience in space.

SCHOOLS NAMED AFTER ELLEN OCHOA

- Ellen Ochoa Middle School—Pasco, Washington
- Ellen Ochoa Learning Center—Cudahy, California
- Ellen Ochoa STEM Academy at Ben Milam Elementary—Grand Prairie, Texas
- Ánimo Ellen Ochoa Charter Middle School—Los Angeles, California
- Ellen Ochoa Prep Academy—Pico Rivera, California
- Ellen Ochoa Elementary—Tulsa, Oklahoma

"I take seriously that part of my career and life," Ellen has said. "For young Hispanic women, there are few well-known women in STEM fields, so it's even more important to let them know about the interesting and rewarding careers that they can pursue."

DID YOU KNOW?

★ Ochoa's parents were born in the United States, while her paternal grandparents were immigrants from Sonora, Mexico.

projectbrainlight.org/blog/birthday-biography-ellen -ochoa?format=amp

★ She was the eleventh director of the Johnson Space Center. She was the center's first Hispanic director and its second female director.

nasa.gov/centers/johnson/about/people/orgs/bios/ochoa.html

★ Ochoa flew in space four times, including missions STS-56, STS-66, STS-96, and STS-110. She logged nearly one thousand hours in orbit.

nasa.gov/centers/johnson/about/people/orgs/bios/ochoa.html

★ Ochoa has received NASA's highest award, the Distinguished Service Medal, and the Presidential

Distinguished Rank Award, which recognizes senior executives in the federal government.

nasa.gov/centers/johnson/about/people/orgs/bios/ochoa.html

★ Ochoa is a Fellow of the American Association for the Advancement of Science (AAAS) and the American Institute of Aeronautics and Astronautics (AIAA). In addition, she has served on several boards and has chaired the Nomination Evaluation Committee for the National Medal of Technology and Innovation.

nasa.gov/centers/johnson/about/people/orgs/bios/ochoa.html

★ Ochoa was inducted into the United States Astronaut Hall of Fame in 2017.

nasa.gov/press-release/two-nasa-astronauts-inducted-into
-us-astronaut-hall-of-fame

★ In 2019, Ochoa was named a Stanford Engineering Hero by her alma mater for her scientific work.

csuitespotlight.com/2021/06/24/astronaut-ellen-ochoa
-officially-a-hero-at-alma-mater-stanford-university/

★ In April 2022, Ochoa took a flag with the logo of Ochoa Middle School in Pasco, Washington, with her aboard the shuttle *Atlantis*. She returned the flag to the school in 2002, where it remains on permanent display.

Ochoa Middle School

★ Ochoa has said the movie *Apollo 13* very closely resembles the real interaction between mission control, engineers on the ground, and the astronauts in orbit.

sandiegouniontribune.com/name-drop-san-diego
/story/2020-05-12/ellen-ochoa-astronaut-nasa-name-drop
-san-diego

★ Hispanic adults make up 17 percent of the workforce but just 8 percent of those working in a science, technology, engineering, or math (STEM) job.

pewresearch.org/science/2022/06/14/many-hispanic
-americans-see-more-representation-visibility-as-helpful-for
-increasing-diversity-in-science/

★ There has been an increase in the share of Hispanic students attending and graduating from college as well as in the share of Hispanic students earning bachelor's degrees in a STEM field (up from 8 percent in 2010 to 12 percent in 2018, according to Pew Research Center analysis of US Department of Education data). Even so, Hispanic students are still underrepresented in STEM degree programs.

pewresearch.org/science/2022/06/14/many-hispanic
-americans-see-more-representation-visibility-as-helpful-for
-increasing-diversity-in-science/

★ As recently as 2020, only 37.8 percent of bachelor's degrees in STEM and 24.2 percent in engineering were awarded to women, and a mere 9.6 percent of engineering bachelor's degrees were awarded to women of color. The proportion of engineering PhDs awarded to women of color is even smaller.

swe.org/research/2021/women-in-engineering-fast-facts/

A NOTE FROM NATHALIE ALONSO

As a kid, I was fascinated by space. I devoured every book about the solar system that I could get my hands on. The volcanoes on the surface of Venus, the Great Red Spot on Jupiter, the rings of Saturn—I was enthralled by all of it.

At one point in my childhood, I thought I would grow up to become an astronomer. However, by the time I took my first astronomy course in college, I had come to realize that I was more of a writer than a scientist. Yet my interest in space never left me, and so I leaped at the chance to write a book about the first female astronaut of Hispanic descent.

As dazzled as I was by space growing up, though, I never once thought about becoming an astronaut. It takes a special person to set such a lofty goal, especially when you come from an underrepresented group. For me, the lesson of Ellen Ochoa's life and career is about the rewards and the magic that happens when you dream big, even when the path for you isn't well defined.

That is a theme with many of the figures featured in the Hispanic Star series and one of the reasons their biographies remain valuable and powerful for new generations. I am honored to contribute Ellen Ochoa's story to this incredible project.

A NOTE FROM HISPANIC STAR

When Hispanic Star decided to join Macmillan and Roaring Brook Press in creating this chapter book biography series, our intention was to share stories of incredible Hispanic leaders with young readers, inspiring them through the acts of those Stars. For centuries, the Hispanic community has made significant contributions to different spaces of our collective culture—whether it's sports, entertainment, art, politics, or business—and we wanted to showcase some of the role models who made this possible. We especially wanted to inspire Latinx children to rise up and take the mantle of Hispanic unity and pride.

With Hispanic Star, we also wanted to shine a light on the common language that unifies a large portion of the Latinx community. *Hispanic* means "Spanish speaking" and frequently refers to people whose origins are from a country where Spanish is the primary spoken language. The term *Latinx*, in all its ever-changing deviations, refers to people of all gender identities from all countries in Latin America and their descendants, many of them already born in the United States.

This groundbreaking book series can be found both in English and Spanish as a tribute to the Hispanic community in our country.

We encourage all of our readers to get to know these heroes and the positive impact they continue to have, inviting future generations to learn more about the different journeys of our unique and charming Hispanic Stars!

THE HISPANIC STAR SERIES

Read about the most groundbreaking, iconic Hispanic heroes who have shaped our culture and the world in this gripping biography series for young readers.

IF YOU CAN SEE IT, YOU CAN BE IT.